Contents

Dedication

This book is dedicated to several people.

To Claire for being my confidant and friend who made me laugh when I was at the lowest emotional point of my life.

To the psychiatrist who finally made a correct diagnosis.

To Rose for her sense of humor and encouraging me to finish the book.

Finally, to my brother Gary who passed away a month before the book was completed. I hope that he would be proud of my accomplishment.

WHO'S STUPID NOW?

DIAGNOSIS: BIPOLAR

A. TONI LE BOSS

outskirtspress
DENVER, COLORADO

Prologue

It is no secret that many famous people, dead or alive, are reported to have experienced mental illness. Most have genius or creative talents. I am sincerely honored to be among them.

To name a few: Patty Duke, Albert Einstein, Carrie Fisher, Mariette Hartley, Sinead O'Connor, Jane Pauley, Jean-Claude Van Damme, Vincent Van-Gogh, Virginia Woolf and Catherine Zeta-Jones.

Introduction

It was 1992 on a cloudy October day in New England. The kind of day that made you want to just crawl under the covers with a good book. I thought of my parents who were both born during that month. It saddened me that they had passed on years before and could not witness what I'd accomplished. I had a comfortable home and it was worth all the years of emotional and mental suffering. They may have felt that it was too extravagant for a single woman. I no longer had to seek their approval. Yet something inside of me felt a sense of guilt. Why should I? Don't I deserve to be happy? These were the thoughts that were going through my head.

I remembered back to my early twenties when I could barely afford a one-bedroom apartment. Thanks to a sizeable inheritance and a profitable job with a telecommunications company, I was on top of the world and living in this beautiful 2,500-square-foot home. Wow. This was my palace. There was a shiny marbled foyer and a matching fireplace in the sunken living room. The master bedroom was enormous and decorated with a canopy bed purchased from Jordan Marsh and I did not spare any expense having it shipped from Florida. It was adorned with the most intricate eyelet lace to match the draperies.

There was even a sitting room outside the bedroom, overlooking the living room and a guest room. Each bedroom had an adjoining bath. The expansive dream kitchen had wall to ceiling cabinets, pull-out shelves and even a hidden step stool.

The large dining room was elevated. The ceilings were high. To my amazement, there were built in vacuum cleaners on each level. What made it so unique was that it was built California style yet I was in New England. It was beyond anything I could have ever imagined being mine. With all of this space, I contacted Ethan Allen and worked with them to furnish and upholster the window treatments to match my brushed pink kitchen cabinets.

Everything was coordinated in Southwestern tones of turquoise, mint green and peach (popular in the 80's).

But it wasn't always this peaceful.

Suddenly the thunder and lightning was so loud that it woke my puppy from his nap. I looked outside the living room window and the rain was coming down in large droplets. I took him out the back sliding glass door for a quick walk. Then the rain started to turn to hail. The puppy's small paws hurt when he walked. I felt his pain, and brought him into the garage where I propped him up on his changing table. I dried him off with a plush towel and then came inside and turned on the weather channel.

The weatherman predicted a heavy snow storm later in the evening. It was arriving early this year. New England weather was so changeable. It was a lot like my mood changes. I put some logs on the fire, turned the jazz radio station on very low, and poured myself a half glass of Merlot. It was not too long before I began to doze off. I may have been dreaming.

1

The Hospital

I awoke in a hospital room in South Florida. The institutional smell of piss was overwhelming. I tried to open my eyes to see where I was but the light from the window was too bright. As I lay there, sweat was pouring down my chest and I felt a powerful ache in my stomach. I wanted to throw up. I started to cough but all that came up was water.

Outside the room, I caught a glimpse of a female figure in uniform. I yelled for her to come inside. "Come here and close the blinds," I demanded. "The sun is shining directly in my eyes and, furthermore, it is fucking hot in this room." "Where am I and how the hell did I get here?" Despite my attempts to end my life the night before, unless I was in Hades, I was alive and not quite ready to "see the light."

The attending nurse replied, "Good morning, Madame, this is just another day in Paradise. Are you feeling any better? Don't despair."

"What the hell are you talking about?" I replied. "I feel like crap and I am hot and dying of thirst."

"Well, unfortunately we had to pump your stomach and

you are on a mild tranquilizer to calm you. There is a pitcher of water right by your bed but I will refresh it for you." The nurse wiped the sleep out of my eyes and took a damp cool towel to clean my chest. "I am sorry but you are a very sick young lady."

"What is this Madame crap?" "I am not a prostitute and you can call me Miss."

"So sorry, miss, but in my country that is how we address our ladies."

I was angry and frustrated because the night before was a just a vague memory. After I took a few hits of a stale joint, I remember going to the medicine cabinet and emptying three different bottles of pills onto the kitchen counter. I tried counting the pills to be absolutely certain there was enough to do the job, but my head was getting cloudy. I hated the pills but I was on a mission. Little did I know that it would become "mission impossible."

I'd tried several times in the past ten years but I was always saved. I did not believe in a supreme being but, if he or she actually existed, this was the time to come through.

What purpose was there for me to be on this earth? I hate pills. It seemed that all shrinks prescribed them because they really didn't know how to get to the root of the problems. I had very little faith in my shrink, Dr. Slickman. According to my family, he came highly recommended as one of the best in the state. Money was no object, because the wealthy side of the family was footing the bill. You know how money talks? Well, there was not much talking going on in the doctor's office. I noticed that he took a lot of notes. He must have been writing his daily journal or bucket list. He may have even been writing a love letter to his mistress.

I believed that no one knew or could feel the pain I was

going through, except perhaps another individual with mental illness. I did not know anyone close to me with the illness, except those who were in a psychotherapy group. For years, I mainly kept to myself and avoided social activities. My family's favorite phrase was "snap out of it." As if it was that simple.

I realize now that because mental illness is a hidden disease, they just did not know how to handle the situation. I didn't know how to help myself either.

After lying for what seemed like hours, I began to get the urge to pee and tried to sit up in the bed, but was too groggy.

The nurse was nowhere in sight. I yelled "Help, I need someone now!" Why doesn't anyone come to help me?" Tears rolled down my face. "I am in pain."

The nurse finally showed up huffing and puffing. "We had an emergency down the hall."

"Well, this is a goddamn emergency too."

"Where are you when I need you?" "I am going to report you to the head of this hospital when I leave." The nurse smiled and then went into the bathroom and got the pan so that I could eliminate. I could not wait, and pee started streaming out from all sides of my asshole. Hell, at least I don't have to clean it up. As they say, "Oh what a relief it is." The nurse changed my sheets, propped up my pillows and said that she was going to give me a short neck and upper back massage.

I would say that made up for the aggravation.

The nurse asked me if I needed anything else.

"A cigarette would be nice."

"Sorry, but you should know that smoking is not permitted in the hospital."

"Yes, but I thought that I was special. Also, in lieu of the way I have been treated so far, it would be the least this hospital can do."

"Now just mind your little self because those are the rules and they cannot be broken."

"Oh yeah" I thought. "I am going to have to work on that."

"In the meantime, dear, I'm right outside if you do need anything else to make you more comfortable until your doctor comes. I'm going to give you this buzzer to press. Please do not be shy."

"She certainly does not know me very well." My moods change like the weather forecast. I can be bright and sunny one minute and cloudy, rainy, and sending out lightning bolts the next.

On the contrary, the sweet nurse was a petite, dark-skinned girl. I was surprised that she had such strong hands. I was jealous of her beautiful Colgate white teeth, sweet angelic voice, and her shiny straight black hair which was pulled back in a neat bun.

Her petite frame, probably not more than 102 pounds soaking wet, was much to be envious of. Her words of comfort were endearing.

She reminded me of the black housekeeper my family employed when I was a child. Her name was Carrie and she was hired to do the house-cleaning, cooking, and occasional baby-sitting. We considered her more like a member of the family. What I remember most was that Carrie bought M&Ms to my brother and me every time she came, because she knew it was our favorite candy.

She had long thin fingers with soft and pliable skin.

They felt warm to the touch. My brother Skippy (named after the peanut butter) and I probably loved Carrie as much as we loved our parents.

I kept falling in and out of sleep and was repeating over and over in my head the things that must have contributed to the decision to end my life.

Was this disease 50% inherited and 50% environmental? Years of therapy did not work. Like most people I knew, I wanted to blame what I thought were the dysfunctional parts of my life.

2

Background

I was born into a middle class Jewish family in the late 40's. My parents named me Toni after the 'home permanent' commercial that was frequently seen on television. Until I was five, we lived in Manhattan in a high rise building facing the Museum of Natural History. Although I was very young, and my memory serves me right, the apartment was very large with floor to ceiling high windows and wide window sills.

A lot about my childhood is hazy. What remains vivid in my mind is that every year we watched the Macy's Day Parade. My Daddy would prop me up on the window sill and hold me tight in his comforting arms while I watched the big floats go by. It was an amazing sight.

There were baton twirlers and hundreds of marching bands. I was so fascinated with the children on floats singing popular show tunes. It was one of the happiest memories of my early childhood. "Wow Daddy, there goes Pluto." I loved doggies and was always asking him, "When will a puppy come to our house?"

Sadly, he replied "Sorry, honey, but they do not allow puppies in apartments."

"What about a kitty?"

He replied, "Someday you will have a kitty, sweetheart." I believed whatever my Daddy told me. He was kind, generous, caring and he would do anything to make the family happy.

I never knew my real ancestry, because my grandparents were not alive when I was born. I was told that they were born in Austria and Germany (which was probably why I had blonde hair and light eyes). My Daddy told me that when his father came to America he had to change his last name. He chose one that did not sound Jewish. Perhaps it was to avoid any anti-Semitism. I did not understand what that meant until I was older. There were actually people who were prejudiced against Jewish people. This was something I did not understand but accepted. It was never a problem for me because I did not have Jewish characteristics or a Jewish name.

My family only attended synagogue on the high holy days and had dinner together on the Jewish New Year and Passover.

It was tradition and not religion. That is the way I was brought up.

Probably the first traumatic event in my life (other than coming out of the womb), was when I turned three and my mother took me to Best & Company on Fifth Avenue to have my hair curled.

You never heard anyone cry so loud when the hot curling iron hit my scalp.

"Please Mommy, Mommy, it hurts. I want to go home, I would scream." She tried over and over again to calm me down, until the people in the store began to get very irritated.

Mommy said, "Don't worry, honey; the nice lady will give you a big balloon when we're finished, if you are a good little girl."

This worked only for that one day. Now mother had to come up with a better solution.

What a surprise when Daddy came home that night. He came to the rescue. In my eyes, he was the best Daddy. His only flaw was that he was rarely home. It was not his fault. He had a very responsible job managing theatres on 42nd street in Manhattan. It was demanding and he worked long hours and was exhausted when he came home. The usual ritual was lying down for a nap, getting up for dinner, watching a little television, and falling asleep. Then my Mother would wake him to go to bed.

It was a sign of the 50's. Maybe things have not changed that much today.

This particular night when he came home, at the dinner table mother began discussing what happened while trying to get a haircut.

He was a very compassionate man and began to think of a way to solve the problem. "Why not bring Toni down to the Max movie theater next week and she can have her hair done by my personal barber and sit it in big barber chair." "Would you like that honey?" (He looked at me and smiled with his big baby blues.) "Yes, yes, Daddy, I can't wait."

My mother smiled showing her approval.

The following week, I went down to the theatre with Daddy. What a great day it was. Not only would I have my hair cut and curled, but I saw a black and white short movie, a cartoon, and two movies starring Shirley Temple.

Daddy bought me two boxes of M&M candy. I even brought home some glossy photos of movie stars that I could hang up in my room or show to friends. Cary Grant, Doris Day and Rock Hudson were among my favorite. From that day on, all of my haircuts were at the theatre, along with the fond memories of sharing time with my father.

Mother always put the extra black and white photos in the bottom of the hutch in the dining room for safekeeping.

She was a neat, orderly and organized person. She liked things to be in place at all times.

Although I do not recall her demanding the same of me or my brother, she must have instilled it in us. Skippy and I have always shown obsessive compulsive behavior. His most annoying habit is when he gets a small bag of garbage filled. Instead of placing it in a can in the garage, he simply cannot wait for the garbage man and transports it to the nearest trash dump. It drives his wife crazy. I obsess about thinking of the next meal that I am going to eat. In addition, I'm always going back to straighten things in my house when they are out of place. Then I wonder why I do this. I live alone and cannot imagine that it would bother my two cats.

In my early years of pre-school, kindergarten, and elementary school, my mother was a stay-at-home domestic. She often went on Parent Teacher Association outings. My father provided well for the family and she never needed to work. In those days, most of the mothers of my friends stayed home.

It was very rare if they didn't. In my mind, it was the right thing for the mother to stay home and care for the children. My mother was not demonstrative of her feelings. She rarely hugged or kissed me. Her way of showing love was to fill my Dale Evans lunch box with goodies and provide all of the material things.

My closest family was Aunt Francine and Uncle Steve who lived in the West Bronx.

Mother and Aunt Francine were sisters. They had a daughter who was nine years older but she was never home. I would hear them talking about how she was mixed up with the wrong crowd, was flunking out of school, and they had to send her to a psychiatrist.

My mother and Aunt Francine would often discuss their

monthly visits to a brother in the mental institution. I never met him. He was apparently institutionalized after his wife died and he was unable to cope with life. They would bring him money to buy cigarettes.

Suddenly I woke up. Wow, that was quite a dream. It seemed endless. Could I manage to get a cigarette? I couldn't get my mind off of the need for oral gratification. I guess that I would have to settle for something to eat instead. I buzzed the nurse.

"Yes miss, can I help you?"

"What do you have to eat in this shit hole?"

"Watch your language."

About fifteen minutes later, she brought some salt free chicken broth and some crackers.

"This is disgusting. Can't they do better than this? I want Chinese wonton. I want my mother's delicious matzo ball soup."

When I finished, I buzzed for the nurse to get the pee pan and refresh the water in the pitcher.

"So, my dear, how was the soup?"

"I could just puke, but I don't want to get it all over my gown."

"Oh my dear, when you get out of here, I promise to make you a special soup from my country. "Do you like fish?"

"If it's not too fishy," I replied.

"Well, it has several different kinds of fish. It is supposed to cure whatever ails you."

"Sounds like Jewish chicken soup to me. As long as there is no gefilte fish in it, perhaps I would eat it."

The nurse replied, "I guarantee it will be delicious, healthy and will make you strong."

"Okay, then, I will humble myself and try it."

"Where were you born?" I asked the nurse.

"Haiti," she replied.

"What is your name?"

"It's Ayida."

"That is quite unique and beautiful. What does it mean?"

"The gift of love." "I guess that my mother wanted me to be a nurse and a caretaker."

I nodded. "Yes, she must have had a sixth sense."

I looked her over. If anyone could charm me, it was going to be Ayida.

"Do you enjoy your job?" I went on.

"Oh my, yes, dear. It is a good opportunity for someone like me. I come from a very poor country and I must support my family of five children. My husband fled the country during a flood and we have never heard from him since. My children are cared for by my elderly aunt and uncle. I only get to visit them once a year."

I became extremely sad and ashamed for thinking that my life was difficult. It is hard to put things in perspective when you are suffering, but if you reflect on what others are going through in their lives, you begin to appreciate what you have and do not take it for granted.

It wasn't long before I fell asleep again and was dreaming about Chinese food. In my dream, I was walking around Chinatown in New York. (Good Chinese food is hard to find in Florida). I looked around to see where most locals were eating and stopped in for some wonton soup, an egg roll, spare ribs, lemon chicken and chicken fried rice. It was extremely delicious and I had plenty left over to take home (in my dream). My fortune cookie said, "When you get to the white of the plate, it is time to stop eating."

3

Who Am I?

As a young child I was chubby with a figure like my father's: a flat backside, high waist, a big abdomen, and ash blonde hair. I had my mother's eyes and small nose. My mother, on the other hand, was petite with dark hair. Although people thought my brother, Skippy, and I looked alike because we had the same coloring; he really was more a combination of both. We were a very quiet family. Conversation was rare. I thought that I inherited genes for being shy and introverted. I did not particularly like my looks. In elementary school, my mother had my hair cut in a "Buster Brown" style which accentuated my round freckled face. I was never popular with the boys.

This disturbed my mother. She thought I was too cute not to try to be more sociable and, against my wishes, insisted that I attend the school dance. I was humiliated and mortified but wanted to please her. It was important to me that my parents were happy; however, the dances were the longest two hours of my life. Who wants to stand on one side of the gymnasium waiting for a boy to approach you? They never did. That was the beginning of my low self esteem and feelings of inferiority.

My obsession with eating came at a very early age. It first was evident when I found my missing pink baby book in the side drawer of the antique desk in the foyer. I was twelve at the time.

There were of locks of my ash blonde hair tied with a baby pink ribbon. My mother wrote, "Toni likes all kinds of foods. Toni cleaned her plate today. Toni eats all of her vegetables." I was amused but was pleased to see that at least it was in my mother's handwriting.

My love for eating continued throughout early childhood. I baked chocolate chip cookies with my Betty Crocker cookie set and when my best girlfriend came over we made the best white tuna fish salad using about one cup of mayonnaise and chopped onions. I can still taste it. During lunch breaks, I walked to the five and dime store with friends and bought as much candy as I could for the 25 cent allowance I received.

Who can forget those wonderful penny candies: Sugar Daddy, Lick-A-Maid, Turkish Taffy, Pez and Chocolate Babies were my favorite. Of course, there were frequent visits to the dentist.

When I came home from school, I'd go out to the playground with swings in the back of the building. There were always a lot of children laughing and having a good time. On the weekends, there was the Good Humor Man.

My mother would say, "Toni, you should get the Italian ice pop."

"I don't want the ice pop. I want the chocolate-covered one with sprinkles." I cried every time until she gave in.

This was one of the things that gave me the most satisfaction.

I envied my brother, Skippy, for a lot of reasons, but most of all because he did not have a weight problem. He could eat all of the burgers and fries he wanted and never gain a pound.

Mother would get angry with him when she prepared a nice balanced meal with chopped meat, boiled white potatoes, string beans and apple sauce. He always turned his nose up and would pick at his food. We never had drinks with dinner. I thought it was a Jewish custom, because when I went to my Christian friends' houses for dinner, they always served iced tea.

By the time my brother was still working on one quarter of his hamburger, I'd consumed everything on the plate.

I could hear him say, "Hey Chubby, when you get to the white of the plate it is time to quit." Where did I hear that before?

I was hurt inside but just looked down and never said a word. My parents avoided the issue. If they were concerned, they kept it to themselves.

4

The Good Ole' Days

Skippy loved to tease me. His favorite game was pushing me down on the floor, placing his legs over my torso and pretending that he was tickling me. He never meant to hurt me, only to torture me. I would laugh, but when it got to be too much I screamed and cried. Daddy would run for the belt and scare Skippy but he never hit him hard. He'd be sent to his room. I always felt bad that he was being punished. No matter what, he was my big brother, and I idolized him. Punishment was not being able to watch television. This was difficult because it was usually turned on 24/7.

Skippy was three years older, a very intelligent and inquisitive child, and frequently got into trouble. I do not remember doing anything that required punishment. Skippy appeared to have no fear and seemed to always find ways to act out. One time, Daddy put away cases of Coke in the hall closet for an upcoming party. Skippy managed to get into the closet and open up all of the bottle caps. It was a rare occasion that Daddy was so enraged.

"Just what do you think you are doing, young man?" he

yelled. That time, Skippy actually felt the belt on his backside and the worst possible punishment was taking away his allowance for three months.

We lived in a high rise apartment building on top of a steep hill. When it snowed, we went sleigh riding down the hill. You had to be very careful or you might land on the sidewalk. It was so much fun. Skippy liked to make snow balls and throw them at people as they walked by. I ignored him and did not want him to get into trouble, but that was unavoidable. He accidentally hit a policeman walking by. The officer was not hurt but took him upstairs to talk to Daddy. Skippy's allowance was taken away for six months. It appeared that money was the only bargaining tool in our house. If you were bad, then your allowance was taken away. I had a full piggy bank.

I was troubled by the fact that I was shy, overweight, got poor grades in school and was unpopular with boys. At the same time, I tried to be kind and generous with everyone I met. Skippy was outgoing, quick-witted, strong and got good grades in school, but he also showed signs of being cold and selfish. We had very different personalities.

Despite these differences, I still felt extreme love for my brother and remember the special times we bonded. On rainy days, when we were stuck inside, we created a special game.

Skippy would take a blanket and two brooms and make a tent in his room. Then he would brew a pot of Lipton tea and get a box of biscuits and break them into small pieces. Then he would put the biscuits into tea mugs, add just the right amount of sugar, and mash them all up. As unappetizing as it may sound to some, we thought it was delicious. Most of all, for me it was a time of sibling love and acceptance.

In those days, doctors made house calls, milk machines were in the basement of the apartment buildings, we walked to the local butcher store to buy meat, we did not have to lock our doors, and we could keep all of our candy on Halloween. Kids hung out in the halls of the building with friends. Saturday nights I was a babysitter for couples in our building.

5

Changes

When I was ten, my life changed dramatically. Carrie had taken sick and passed away. The family grieved for a very long time. My mother had relied a lot on Carrie's help and seemed to feel lost and alone despite all the friends she had. She became completely reclusive. She stopped calling friends and had difficulty getting out of bed. After several weeks, her behavior became very odd. It was as if she was becoming paranoid. One morning when I was walking around the house, she looked at me and gasped, "Why are you wearing my clothes, Toni?" I didn't know what she was talking about.

"I am not wearing your clothes, Mother," I replied.

The bizarre behavior continued for about a month, and then Skippy and I were told that she was not well and would have to go to the hospital. She was having a "nervous breakdown." That terminology was foreign to us and very frightening. We were also told that we were going to be sent to a boarding school. I thought I was being sent away forever, and did not understand why Daddy or a relative could not take care of us.

The following day, Daddy brought us to his sister's home in Greenwich, Connecticut.

It was large with four white columns on the outside. There were two statues of tigers on each side of the house, as if they were standing guard and not allowing anyone inside. It was cold and uninviting. "Is this where we are staying, Daddy?" I asked.

"No darling. You are going to a wonderful school which you will both love. Daddy has to go to work, but it will not be for long."

Aunt Anna (Daddy's sister) and Uncle Maurice did not have any children of their own.

They were very wealthy and even had their own chauffer, butler and a full kitchen and cleaning staff.

They were footing the bill for the school.

A black man in uniform opened the front door to the house.

"Hello, Miss Toni and Master Skippy," he said. "I am pleased to meet you. My name is Theodore."

All of this was so overwhelming to me.

Then I overheard my Aunt whisper to my uncle, "I could have predicted that something like this was going to happen one day. You know how emotionally weak that woman always was. Just look at the family she came from. They are all crazy. I never understood what my brother saw in her anyway."

She continued, "If it wasn't for the fact that I love my brother so much, I would have told him years ago how I felt. He has been blind all of these years, but he loved his children and they should not have to suffer. We will enroll them at that wonderful Berry Lawn boarding school."

Tears rolled down my face, but at the same time I felt relieved not to be around my mother while she was in a "crazy" state of mind.

When we arrived at Berry Lawn we were met by the Headmaster. He was a tall, grey-haired distinguished looking man.

"Welcome, children. We are so pleased to have you at Berry Lawn. I know that you will be happy during your stay here. Please let me show you around."

His soft voice and kind words were encouraging. The surroundings were quaint and there were beautiful large Maple trees throughout the grounds. The main house was large and looked like a southern mansion.

It was painted in a beautiful colonial blue. There were separate living quarters for the boys and girls. The boys' was Colonial style and the girls' looked like a Victorian doll house.

There were four classroom buildings where separate subjects were taught. Each was a different color, which made it easy to distinguish one from the other. It was a charming New England school. Maybe it would not be too terrible.

In the sleeping quarters everyone had a private bedroom and bath. Classes were small—with ten students—which meant we were able to get a lot of attention. Things were going fine, but after nine months, I was homesick so I immersed myself in my studies.

My favorite class was wood-working and I made a mahogany colored jewelry box lined in red velvet which was inscribed with my mother's initials. I showed it to my teacher.

"When my mother comes home," I said. "I am going to give this to her and I hope it will cheer her up."

"Oh my dear child," the teacher replied, "you are a thoughtful little girl."

I looked forward to evenings when we were given a quarter to buy candy.

Much to my surprise, after the first week, a really cute boy named Bruce started flirting with me. He played the guitar and every night sat by one of the trees singing "Kisses Sweeter than Wine."

He was the first boy who ever showed interest in me and I was smitten. A few months later, when no one was around, he surprised me. He came around the corner, handed me some wild flowers, and kissed me.

It was not just a peck but a long wet kiss. I had never experienced that before and I had butterflies in my stomach. He was very easy to talk to. We were up for hours discussing our thought and our dreams. Over the year our friendship grew.

Bruce told me that he came to Berry Lawn because his parents had gone through a divorce and felt that they could not give him the kind of attention that he needed.

He was thirteen and already knew that he would join the military when he turned sixteen. It was not easy to talk about why Skippy and I had to be sent away to school but I confided in him and he was very sympathetic.

We locked pinkies and made a promise to each other that we would keep in touch when we left Berry Lawn.

We were at Berry Lawn for a year. Mother was released from the hospital, and we were finally going home. I packed and said goodbye to the friends I had made. Leaving Bruce was one of the hardest things I had to do. I felt "puppy love" for the first time and had grown attached to him.

The memory of having a boy show interest was something I would hold in my heart forever. Daddy came to pick us up and said, "It might take mother a lot of time to adjust to being home again. I know it has not been easy for you, but just know that we love you very much." He was right. We all had to adjust. Friends wanted to hear everything about the experience at Berry Lawn. Mother was very slow getting back to herself. She was on heavy medication and stayed close to home. She chose not to call any of her friends and rarely went out.

Things went from bad to worse. Daddy suffered a heart attack. He was rushed to the hospital and was there for over two weeks being treated.

The doctors told him he would have to stop smoking the four packs of Chesterfield cigarettes a day and change his diet from red meat to low fat meats.

That would be a death sentence right there. The day he was expected to be released, he suffered a second heart attack. They were unable to save him.

Mother came home and gave us the tragic news. "My dear," she cried, "Daddy will not be coming home. They tried everything to save him." I was only twelve years old, and I felt it was the worst day of my life. Skippy was out with his friends and would get the news later.

No one realized how much it would affect Skippy. He appeared to be in shock when he heard the news. At the funeral, all the relatives went up to him and said, "Take care of your mother and sister because you are now the man in the family." He did not show much emotion but I was sure he was crying on the inside.

6

Doctor's Arrival

I awoke with a pounding headache and buzzed for the nurse. "I must have a glass of cold water and something to calm my nerves right now."

"I'll check with the doctor, my dear. I'll be right back." She brought some water with two Tylenol caplets.

"God Damn," I said. "Don't they have anything stronger than that?"

I heard the sound of someone removing the chart from the back of the door. The two began to speak and shortly thereafter, in walked my psychiatrist, Dr. Slickman. He smiled his usual sly grin, despite the fact that he looked pretty dapper in his midnight blue pinstripe suit, white shirt, and navy blue tie. I may not have liked his cool demeanor but had to admit he was a good looking guy and had nice-smelling after shave lotion. It was a refreshing contrast to the medicinal odor in the hospital.

He stared down at me with his piercing brown eyes, eyebrows raised, and in an impassioned tone, whispered in my ear, "What did you think you were doing? What a stupid girl you are!"

No one was going to call me stupid, and especially not my doctor. I was devastated. Didn't he realize how desperate I was to try to commit suicide? He was a doctor showing very little comfort when I needed it. I could not take his "tough love" attitude.

I looked back up at him and said, "Dr. Slickman, I do not think I can talk to you now. I am not feeling well. Please leave."

He mumbled something under his breath, took some notes, shook his head and calmly walked out of the room.

I felt that opportunity was staring me in the face now.

7

The Annex

The next morning, they released me from the general part of the hospital and I was led through the metal doors of the psychiatric ward which was commonly referred to as the "Annex." Two twelve foot high by twelve foot wide locked metal doors separated two wings of the hospital. Outside the doors was a security cage where two guards watched the ward twenty-four hours a day. At the cage, I was greeted by a large social worker who looked like an elementary school teacher, with gray hair pulled back in a twist and wide-rimmed glasses.

Along with her was a handsome blonde doctor. He introduced himself as Dr. Rosen and shook my hand. "I am your new doctor, Toni. We will be spending a lot of time together and I hope you will be comfortable in your new surroundings."

Was he kidding? The Annex looked like a scene out of the movie "One Flew over the Cuckoo's Nest."

"Come this way," the social worker said, in a deep and throaty voice. "I am Nurse Hatchet. We are going to get you into a gown, give you some meds and then in a little while you will go to group therapy."

Sarcastically, I thought, "Great! They just finished pumping my stomach to get rid of meds and they are going to start all over again." However, Dr. Rosen was as good looking as a movie star.

I was already afraid that I may develop a fatal attraction. My past history of falling for the wrong men, made me think about why it is referred to as "Mental" illness. Paranoia was setting in and I was feeling a little dizzy. I needed to lie down. Looking around, I saw men and women of all shapes and sizes walking with dazed looks on their faces. There was a guy with his hospital gown worn backwards.

A girl was screaming "No more meds, no more meds," over and over again! Nurses were trying to pull patients out of their beds. It was horrible.

There was no way that I could be as sick as these people. For several days, the whole scene was so upsetting that I had no appetite, which seemed like a positive thing at the time. When my mother came to visit perhaps I would have something to be proud of. I stayed in bed until Dr. Rosen showed up. Our sessions were short but I sure did enjoy looking at him.

He appeared to be frustrated with me because he would say things like, "Toni, if you want to get better you are going to have to interact more with me as well as in group therapy."

I was severely depressed and catatonic at first. All I wanted to do was hide my head under the covers and sleep. My daily activity was waiting for family members to visit but they did not come. It reminded me of summer camp waiting for parents' visiting day. It was the most important day of the eight weeks I was there. Waiting and waiting for that special day. Now I was in a hospital and felt lost, alone and unloved. Skippy only visited when I had to sign checks so none of my bills would be late. Mother and Aunt Francine never came to visit because they did not drive and were hoping that Skippy would take them, which never happened.

He wanted nothing to do with them. He was not interested in anything but his immediate family.

My mother and aunt could be very difficult too. They were both needy. Mother was not emotionally or physically well and my aunt was protective of her and over-demanding. They had few friends and no other family lived close by. Also, I suspected that everyone was sick and tired of me being sick and tired. They had been through this too many times before with hospital after hospital. They were getting older, perhaps overwhelmed, and had little hope that I would recover. However, I thought that I needed their love and support to get well.

After about a month, I was approached by one of the female patients. She was a woman in her 40's with a beautiful smile and sparkling eyes.

"Hi, I'm Clara and you look like you can use a friend."

I still had difficulty getting out of bed, but her words of kindness were convincing.

"I noticed you always sleeping or sitting in the corner, and I feel sorry for you. You really should try to get up and go to group therapy. It helps. I promise you that you will feel a lot better about yourself. Jump into the shower and come to group."

The concept of group therapy was intimidating. It was not easy to sit in a circle, looking at a bunch of strange faces, and telling your life story. It was hard enough to open up to the doctor.

I thought about how the people who go to Alcoholic Anonymous meetings must feel. It took quite a while before I could look people in the eyes and tell them my thoughts and feelings. But I knew that it was part of the program and eventually I would have to. It turned out to be better than sleeping in bed all day.

Clara also made sure that I ate something and participated in some of the other activities. She became a wonderful and comforting friend.

She was a great listener, especially compared to those tiresome meetings with the doctor. She was able to motivate me to join the dance class and start drawing in arts & crafts. Clara's kindness and friendship were a turning point in my recovery. Despite being in the hospital for different reasons we knew that ours was a match made in heaven. Clara was there for anxiety, and I suffered from depression. What we had in common is that we both thought our doctors were cute.

8

Relationships

One day in group, I opened up about Dr. Slickman who said that I was stupid for trying to commit suicide. At the time, I was in a helpless state of mind. I felt as if I was losing my mind. There were quite a few in the group that felt the same. The facilitator of the group assured me that I was not going crazy but experiencing the effects of a disease called manic depression.

She went on to explain that it was not something to be ashamed of and can be treated with medication and the proper ongoing treatment. The causes were not really known but usually they were a combination of heredity and environment.

I was convinced that my family history of mental illness, the loss of my father at an early age, dealing with my home environment, and personal insecurity, were the causes of my manic depression. My relationships with men and disappointments added to the illness.

I decided to wait before going into more detail about each and every one of the men with whom I had affairs. I was hoping that the doctor could find the right medication to stabilize me before I had to spit my guts out.

My goal was to be released from the Annex as quickly as possible. That was not going to be as easy as I thought. First, Dr. Rosen prescribed a book about understanding the illness and I was told to read a few pages per day. Unlike my mother, who read a book a week, the love of reading was not something I inherited. I had a problem focusing and concentrating. It was so difficult to retain what I was reading and I had to reread each paragraph twice. I thought it ironic that I enjoyed writing and often wrote poems when I was feeling depressed.

> **The wind blew the leaves from the trees away**
> **While raindrops came down my window today**
> **Then turned into snowflakes by the end of the day**
> **And there was sunshine to melt them away.**
> **Then there were sunflowers.**

9

College

In the annex that night when I awoke, my heart was racing. I stared at the clock; it was 3:00 a.m. I realized that I was only dreaming, but it seemed so real.

I was sweating and got up to go to the bathroom and filled my cup with water. I drank about half a cup when my hands began to shake. The cup dropped to the floor. I took a towel and dried up the water and got back into bed.

What had happened just then? I made an assumption that it was a reaction to the drugs I was taking but was afraid to let the nurse know. I simply got back into bed and fell asleep.

It was 1965 and I was with my mother on the way to the university.

We arrived in Miami and drove across the I-395 Bridge. It was so clean and beautiful with the crystal clear water (unlike the dirty streets of New York City). I had only seen it in post-cards before, or travel magazines, and I was in awe. We checked into a hotel on Miami Beach for a few days before my registration at the University of Miami. I was scared and excited at the same time. I was unsure if it would be easy to make friends or if

I would be liked. My mother tried to assure me that everything would work out. "Honey, everything is going to be just fine. Remember, Skippy will be close by."

That was small comfort. When was he ever there for me? In the meantime, I was just enjoying the scenery, the tropical environment and the smell of fresh cut grass.

We spent days enjoying the beach. I wanted to get a tan by the time I arrived on campus, but instead I got a terrible third degree burn because I sat with my sun reflector and doused myself with baby oil and iodine. When my skin got dry and crispy, I enjoyed peeling it off. Then I would take after-tan lotion and put it all over me. I don't think anyone knew about skin cancer in those days.

We bought really cute fashionable clothes like halter tops and bell bottom pants. We ate Reuben sandwiches and pickles at the local deli where they put baskets of Danish with a bowl of sour pickles and coleslaw on the tables. I watched how the seniors would wrap the leftovers in their napkins and put them in their purses. I wondered if I would ever do that when I got older.

When I awoke from my dream the next morning, I was late for breakfast. I was disappointed that they did not have any baskets with Danish but I settled for a bowl of corn flakes. When group began, Dr. Rosen arrived and it was my day to speak about something significant that happened in my life.

That was opening up a very big can of worms. Okay, I thought. Let's start with the day I entered the registration office. Clara was all ears. "Would you believe that I had to take a Remedial Reading class because my reading scores on the entry tests were unsatisfactory? I felt so stupid and humiliated."

My friends knew that I never wanted to attend college but it was mother who insisted. Your father saved his whole life for you to go to college," she'd say, "It was his dream." In my heart and mind, I wanted to go to Katherine Gibbs Secretarial School in the Manhattan.

I was a much better typist than a student and had worked every summer since high school at a temporary agency. My mother refused and said, "It would be best for you to go to the university and be close to Skippy." Since there was an age difference, Skippy and I rarely saw each other. There was one time when our sorority got together with his fraternity for a party and he introduced me to a fraternity brother. We got pinned which meant we were going steady and dated for a while. I felt special. I can still smell the musk cologne he wore and his great kisses. I was having fun until he started flirting with one of my sorority sisters, and cheated on me. He married her after college.

One time, I was approached by a gorgeous blonde blue-eyed football player and he asked me out. I remember how excited I was. To have a football player interested in me was awesome. Yellow was my favorite color because it reminded me of sunflowers, and I put on my best yellow bell bottom outfit. He stood me up. My roommate said, "You know he was Catholic and probably found out you were in a Jewish sorority." I was not religious and was feeling rejected, but it was not long before other nice guys were asking me out.

"Wait," said one of the guys in the back, "you mean that your mother spent all of that money to send you to a private college and you goofed off?"

"Well, I guess you can say that, but I don't think it was completely my fault. I was very young and immature and she did not give me any guidance."

"Gee, I would have given anything to go to college."

I grew flushed and embarrassed. Was I being ungrateful? Should I have tried harder to succeed?

In my freshman year, I barely got by academically. I skipped class a lot and no one seemed to notice because classes were held in large auditoriums. I always sat way in the back so I could make a quick getaway. There were times when they did not even have a live professor and the class was taught on a movie screen. I was very bored.

When it came time to take exams, I stayed up all night and crammed. So did most of my fellow classmates. There was no such thing as the internet for reference. To do a paper, I would go to the library, find a National Geographic Periodical and paraphrase. Even though my reading level was low, I was pretty successful at turning in a good paper which would earn me at least a B. My test scores were always very low and I was on academic probation all through my junior year. Finally by the first half of my senior year, I managed to have an average of C and I only needed to do a student-teacher internship to graduate.

It was 1967 and Skippy got drafted to Vietnam right after he got married.

I began to have nightmares. None of my friends believed that a Jew would be drafted. He was not lucky enough to have "flat feet," which would have automatically eliminated him from the Army. He had just gotten married the year before and it was a difficult time for the family. I feared for his life and cried all the time worrying about him. What would my future be like? How was I going to survive after college and where would I live? I was feeling lost and alone.

My sorority sisters were all excited about graduation and I was dreading the day. After all, they had families who loved and supported them. I was going to be out in the world on my own.

My mother had problems too. She did not know how to cope and the only thing we had in common was that we both were suffering from low self esteem and emotional insecurity.

Late one afternoon, while leaving art class, I opened the classroom door and my books fell to the ground. My hands began to tremble uncontrollably. I dropped to the ground sobbing. There was no one around at the time. When I managed to pick myself up off the ground, I hurried over to the Administration Building where I knew the secretary to the president.

When the receptionist saw what state I was in, she called out to the back office. "Come quick, please, I have a young lady who needs some help. What's wrong, honey?"

I felt helpless and unable to speak. I looked wide-eyed into her face. They took one of my books and found my name inside. They rushed me to the nearest psychiatric hospital for observation. They contacted my mother and she took the first available plane out of JFK. The next evening she stood in front of me crying. "Oh, my poor dear, what have they done to you?" I was catatonic. I only glared into her sad glassy eyes.

I remember how I cried when there was no time to have my sorority sisters come to say goodbye, but I was in no condition to have a farewell party.

We flew home in two days with two week's worth of depression medication, and some valium. My mother took a valium on the plane ride home.

With only the second half of my senior year left, I wondered if this was a subconscious way of getting back at my mother for insisting I attend college.

When you think about all of the possibilities, you realize how very complicated the disease of mental illness is. It can strike at any time and become one very toxic cocktail.

1. A tumultuous environment
2. A traumatic event

3. A death
4. Heredity
5. All of the above

By the time I finished telling the story about my break-down, one of the guys got up, came over, placed his hand on my shoulder and said, "And here I thought you were just a spoiled brat!"

I went on with the story. The next few months at home were difficult. I was seeing a renowned psychiatrist. I took a bus from the west side of the city to the upper eastside. I re-member walking up in trepidation to the steps to the brown-stone building. The visits did not appear to be helping. I was completely paranoid all of the time.

Instead of taking the bus home, I decided to walk. I imag-ined that people were following me but the police were pro-tecting me. I saw manila envelopes with the number 44 on the upper left hand corner and thought they contained secretive government information that had to be placed in the closest mailbox by a particular time each night.

It was a living nightmare, but I would not tell anyone be-cause I was afraid they might send me back to the hospital. To this day, whenever I see the number 44, it haunts me. Some taxi cabs are 444-4444 and rental cars in Florida begin with a 44. The number 44 appears in Mark Twain's literary works and the essence of the numerology number 44 is a focus on ef-ficient and conscientious business building. I may not build a future business, but perhaps my winning lotto ticket with the number 44 would come in so I could donate lots of money to the Mental Health Association.

I have diverted from the topic and will continue.

After several months of little improvement, mother was at

her wit's end. She called Skippy and his wife to come up from Florida to help place me in a psychiatric hospital.

They committed me to a State Hospital on the west side of the city. Most of the time, I spent days just sitting in the corner in a catatonic state.

I do remember a sweet young male attendant who tried his best to talk to me and befriend me. He was kind and cute. No matter how hard they tried, none of the staff could get me to talk. The next step was to try electronic shock treatments along with a heavy dose of medication. I must have had six or seven treatments until I spent my maximum allowed time (according to the Baker Act). Then I was sent home.

10

Moving to Florida

The doctors suggested a change of environment and Skippy and his wife came back to relocate us to Florida. I would have to continue treatment there immediately but at least I would be closer to the rest of the family. We were moved into a one bed-room garden apartment north of Fort Lauderdale. I was then placed into another hospital in Coral Ridge where I received intense psychotherapy along with continued heavy doses of medication. Like the New York Hospital, I was only allowed to be there for a maximum of three months. By the time I left, I was talking.

I had appointments with Dr. Slickman as an outpatient at the State Hospital. There were a lot of male patients that looked like big apes walking around a yard outside. Fortunately, they were pretty harmless. I guess they were on a lot of meds too. When I met with Dr. Slickman, his cold demeanor turned me off. I could not wait for the hour session to be over. To make it a little easier for me he never asked many questions. This went on for years. The only thing I got out of these visits was a lot of pills to stabilize my mood swings and relax my nerves. I thought that I must be overdosing because I felt like a walking zombie. I was barely functioning. I walked around in a perpetual state of confusion.

Finally, during one visit, Dr. Slickman began to delve into my family history. I told him how my mother had suffered a breakdown when I was ten, and that my uncle was in an institution since his wife died when they were very young. He took lots of notes and said we would talk more during the next visit.

Living with my mother was not easy or fun. I always hoped things would get better but they never did. She was in a continual state of depression and suffered from chronic bronchitis. She refused to see a doctor. It was time for me to begin doing something productive and my secretarial skills came in handy. I managed to work at low stress jobs.

When I got off work, I would come home and secluded myself in the house. I had virtually little social life. I would only accept dinner invitations from very close friends that knew my state of mind. Mother had a difficult time dealing with her own life. She was basically depressed and bedridden all of the time. As I began improving, I did my best to be sure she ate decent meals. I did the laundry and ironed clothes for work. I did not like cleaning house and only did some light housekeeping. On occasion, when we did go out, she would suffer spells where she would continuously cough up phlegm. People would stare and it was very embarrassing for both of us. It was a sad, stressful, and extremely and overwhelming.

During one session, Dr. Slickman said, "Your mother is your real problem. Getting away from her would be the best thing for you."

Why would he say such a cruel thing? I did not understand. All I wanted to remember was my childhood when she was well and vibrant. At a very early age, I could always depend on her. She was a kind, generous mother. She was there when we needed her. She put Vicks Vapor Rub on my chest when I had a cold. She bought me nice toys, dolls and clothes. She thought I was beautiful. I was proud of her petite stature. No other mother had a natural white streak running through the top and on the left side of her mahogany-colored bouffant.

She dressed in beautiful tailor-made Kimberly Knit suits. She was everything a daughter could ask for.

But that was only reality until I was twelve. Then it all changed. My mother was never the same after my father died. I had deep feelings of anger and resentment because my mother was depressed. I was beginning to realize why I hated my life.

There were those weekend visits to her sister in the Bronx. They were so mundane, but my mother had nothing else to look forward to and I wanted to please her. We would get on the D train heading north, get out on the Grand Concourse and walk to her apartment house. I hated the fact that it was across the street from a grave site. It was morbid.

All day we played gin rummy and watched the news on Channel 2. We watched my aunt's favorite variety show while we ate her predictable dinner of hamburger, green beans, boiled potatoes and apple sauce. The singers and dancers were corny. I hated the sound of "a one and a one and a two" that the host would say in a sing song way. I wanted to leave so badly. This was a Sunday ritual and I think mother looked forward to it. I had no choice. We were family.

When I was alone in the city, I was very self indulgent. I ate too much and shopped compulsively with money that my mother would willingly give me.

She was always very generous with money, but I would have preferred that we go shopping together. I felt neglected and unloved. My friends were always going shopping with their mothers. I looked for every way to mask my sadness and desire to be loved. Monthly, I went to the Plaza restaurant and ate in the beautiful restaurant across from the lobby area. The tables were adorned with white linens and fine china. I couldn't wait to have the finely chopped salad with turkey, ham, Swiss cheese and Thousand Island dressing made right at the table. I was a poor little rich girl pretending to be a princess.

Mother hated to cook but she loved going to the Stage Deli. She would go up to the front of the line and act as if she was someone important to get a seat. I did not think it was funny but it worked every time. "Blimpie's" restaurant was on the first floor of the apartment house where we lived on the west side of 55th street. I was a frequent 'tuna fish on a sub' customer. I tried to fill the emotional holes with food and material things. It worked for a while.

I loved shopping for sales. I walked for hours in high heeled shoes, starting at 57th & fifth and making it down to 34th street to Macy's.

I would take a very slow walk back home, stopping at some of my favorite stores like Chandler's Shoe Store. They had the most fashionable shoes. I loved browsing when I wasn't buying. Then I would go past Peck & Peck and admire their sweater sets.

I also had a fetish for ironing clothes. Our apartment was small and the board was always open in the kitchen area. It drove my mother crazy. I ironed listening to Johnny Mathis records and sang along. It had been my therapy before going off to high school.

There were so many emotions to deal with.

My mother's love was possessive and conditional. If I did not agree with her opinions, then I was not perceived as being good.

As much as I tried to understand my mother's hurt and sadness, I longed for her to be strong and healthy. It was too much of a codependent and destructive relationship.

Perhaps if my grandparents were alive, I would have learned more about what my parent's lives were like growing up. I wanted desperately to understand my family roots.

11

My Daddy

I had my father for a very short time. Twelve is too young to lose your daddy. Talking about him in group therapy was a lot easier. When I thought of him, only good things came to mind. I could see his smiling round face and sparkling blue eyes. He was such a very kind man who adored everybody. He worked long hours, but occasionally on weekends, he would take me and Skippy to the theater downtown or the one in Yonkers to see a movie. Sometimes he would bring a movie reel home and we would invite some friends over to watch cartoons. The time we spent with Daddy was quality more than quantity.

I will always cherish the moments and remember him dearly. I wonder how the loss at an early age has impacted my life. Although I have accepted it, I am also aware of how difficult it was for my mother. He was 55 when he passed and she was only 50.

Our lives were never the same. To keep busy, I encouraged her to try part time work. She reluctantly went to Bloomingdales. After one week, she complained that standing on her feet hurt the spider veins in her ankles. I too have spider veins. Losing Daddy was a pain we shared, along with our spider veins.

In the late 70's, at a family funeral, Skippy and I were told by relatives that our parent's marriage was not as happy as people thought. They were married twenty-three years and stayed together for me and Skippy. This was common for those years.

My aunt (his sister) claimed that is why my father suffered a heart attack. Skippy and I looked at each other in shock. We never even saw them fight. We were aware that mother was jealous of the relationship Daddy had with his sister. Everyone knew how close they were. Sometimes people even made remarks that they looked like lovers. We were very young and did not know if there were any problems. We never suspected anything. Sleeping in separate twin beds was a common occurrence as far as we were concerned.

"Wake up from your nap, Toni. Come on now," announced Nurse Hatchet. It is time for lunch and your favorite, tuna fish, is on the menu." That cheered me up!

After lunch and meds, Nurse Hatchet turned on some Neil Diamond music. It happened to be a song I really liked. I sang out loud, "Holly, holly, holy dream, dream of only me. Come on, Clara, it's time to join in and dance." We rocked to the music for about one half hour and then called it a night.

I began to fall into a deep sleep. I was on a beautiful isolated island with a sexy hippie guy who swept me off my feet. When we reached the island, we took our clothes off and hung them on the branch of a tree and made love on the beach from dawn to sunset. But this was real. It happened when I was thirty and I was in love.

While I waited for Dr. Rosen to arrive for my daily session, I did some arm stretching exercises. It took ten repetitions of five stretches to really get me going. Then I took my shower and got ready for breakfast. I had progressed in one month's time.

I was also famished and Clara was glad to see that I was getting my appetite back.

After breakfast, Clara confided in me about the problems she was experiencing with her marriage. "My husband is a couch potato," she sighed. "Even worse, we have not had sex in ten years."

"Oh my," I exclaimed, "I cannot possibly imagine going without sex for that many years." You could see how frustrated, horny and lonely she was.

Clara resorted to having an affair with her telephone repairman (not unusual for the 70's). When her husband found out, he threatened to leave her. She did not want a divorce because they had a ten-year-old boy who is the love of her life. Her husband said that the only way he would stay married to her was if she got some psychiatric help. A minimum of one month in the Annex was prescribed.

She hoped that Dr. Greene would help her (in the clinical sense). "Come on, girls, it's time for your meds," said Nurse Hatchet.

I detested standing on the line with twenty crazies in front of me. Everybody had their heads down waiting patiently for a fix.

Three times a day, we waited for two pills in a tiny white cup that was supposed to make us better, but it only made me numb.

Clara was engaged in a conversation with one of the guys across the room. I heard loud laughter and saw tears streaming down her face. I assumed they were tears of joy and was pleased. I could not feel the same sense of joy and wondered if I ever would. Then suddenly I saw an accident about to happen and yelled out to her. "Watch out, Clara, Jonathan is about to attack you!"

"What do you mean, Toni?"

"He's running clear across the room with his arms in the air and he's coming in your direction like a madman! Where is the staff when you need them?"

At that moment, Nurse Hatchet came from behind the nurses' station and said, "Just what do you mean by that statement, young lady?"

"I did not mean to be disrespectful, Nurse Hatchet, but Jonathan is panicking and looks like he's about to attack Clara."

"Okay, just sit down and I'll take care of him."

As Nurse Hatchet came out of the nurses' station, her shoe slipped on some water which had spilled on the floor, and there was a loud clumping noise which practically made the walls shake. It took two fairly large attendants to lift her back up. She gained her composure and ran over to where Jonathan was standing.

They grabbed his arms and brought them around to his back. Another attendant dropped him to the floor. They gave him a shot and a few minutes later he was quiet. Clara and I just looked at each other from opposite ends of the room smirking, shrugging our shoulders and giggling.

12

Beware of Greeks

The doctor prescribed lithium. The drug has side affects which, for me, included diarrhea, weight gain and drowsiness. None of these are pleasant. Having diarrhea speaks for itself. The last thing I needed to do was gain weight. It did not take long for the pounds to come back when I started the medication. Also, I cannot remember a day when I could keep my eyes open past 9:30 p.m. It can be very embarrassing when you are out on a date.

My dream brought me back to one particular event in the early 1970's. I needed to get out for the night. I was headed for a dance on Miami Beach where all of the singles go.

After rummaging through my closet, I found an old black sequined top, shimmering pants, light black panty hose to cover my spider veins and fashionable high heel shoes. It was a hot and humid night but if it meant meeting a guy, I wanted to look smashing and was willing to sweat.

It was important for me to make up for all those elementary school days when none of the boys asked me to dance.

The song "Last chance, last dance, last Romance, tonight"

was blasting. I did not care who was watching; I just started swirling around by myself. Then, suddenly, I was approached. He was something out of a romance novel. He put his hand out to greet me as he said, "May I have this dance, beautiful lady?"

He was gorgeous. Over 6' tall with dark shiny brown hair, large brown eyes that sparkled, beautiful white teeth and a charming accent." I was not sure. It sounded Greek to me. And so he was. He complimented my choice in shoes.

It felt like 'love at first sight'. We danced for what felt like hours. Then he asked me if I wanted to see where he lived. It is a nice room in a home connected to a Greek family. "It's not much but I am very comfortable there and I think you will like it." I was a little shy at first, but being a lonely risk-taker I replied, "Sure, I would love to see your home." He told me that he was from a very small fishing village in Greece but left his traditions behind.

He was not kidding. During the next four years, I learned about polygamy, partner swapping, and the local nudist colony. I was living a promiscuous life and, of course, my mother and aunt were completely clueless.

My mother wanted to know where I went all night. "I met a nice Greek guy at a dance."

"Oh, that is wonderful news. All those years of going to dances as a young child and never getting asked to dance. Perhaps it is a mitzvah (blessing)."

It was months before my family insisted on meeting him. They became curious and concerned. He was not Jewish and was from a foreign culture. I assured them that he was very friendly and trustworthy. I was in good hands.

I arranged for a meeting one evening. It did not go as planned. "You said he was friendly, but do you know what he did, exclaimed my Aunt? He shook my hand and placed his middle finger in my palm. That means he was making a pass at me."

It was so ridiculous that I did not even respond to her accusation. Either she was jealous of our relationship because she had not been with a man for over ten years or she just did not like him.

No matter what my family thought, this was a man I could imagine spending my whole life with.

On Sunday mornings, I could not wait to leave my mother's house very early in the morning. I would buy bagels and the Sunday paper and bring it to his place.

It did not matter to me that he had made love to someone else the night before. He would say it had nothing to do with the way he felt about me and I believed him. He would never leave me alone during all of the important holidays like Christmas and New Year's Eve.

As far as I knew, I was the only one who came and left with him to the sex swapping parties. I tried to swap only one time but got sick to my stomach. He never forced me to continue and I pretended to have my period. I would just find one of the girls who was alone and talk until he was finished for the evening. It was difficult not to be jealous when he went with other women, but he still was my man.

I clearly remember the day he told me he was buying a fold down camper that would fit on the top of his car. "Now we are all set to go to the nudist colony on the weekends." It was fortunate for me that Greek men like chubby women. I had gained about thirty pounds after taking lithium. The first time we went, we were greeted at the gate by a completely nude man on a bicycle. His balls were hanging on each side of his seat. I turned my head away and giggled so hard, I thought I would pee in my pants (prior to removing them).

"Welcome to Camp Sunrise," he exclaimed with his big white crooked smile. Make yourselves at home. Park in the lot on the side of the camp and you can undress right there." I looked over to the right where there was a group of women playing volley ball. They were stark naked. One woman had boobs the size of watermelons. I knew that I would be out of place with my flat chest but my boyfriend did not seem to mind. I slowly removed my top.

That is when he affectionately looked at me and said, (Peek-a-boo in his heavy Greek accent).

Life was good and I was extremely happy. Those were the days when I began to spend money recklessly and my credit card bills became astronomical.

My boyfriend was mechanically gifted and took a course in Computer Technology. He was not lazy and I was proud of his accomplishments. So many immigrants slacked off and just collected benefits from the government. He was proud and a hard worker.

The following month he became an American citizen. Then he shocked me by saying, "I have applied for a job on the West Coast. A soon as I am settled, I will send for you." I waited but he never called. When I tried to call him, his phone number had been disconnected. I did not want to admit that I was warned, and just cried for weeks. My life had to change for the better.

13

Giving Up Baby

In 1976, six weeks after my boyfriend left, I found out that I was pregnant, but there was no way to get in touch with him. He would not have any part of the baby anyway. He always said that he did not want children. I was too young to take care of a child. Telling my family was out of the question.

Being a single mother was something I could not imagine. I was not stable or mature enough to bring up a child alone. I certainly did not want to go to full term and put a baby up for adoption. The only option was to abort but it was illegal in Florida.

I borrowed money from an old friend and contacted Planned Parenthood in New York City.

Then I called my oldest girlfriend who met me at the airport. We went directly to the clinic. The doctor said, "You have an infection. It must be cleared up before the procedure can take place."

I was so depressed. I imagined a beautiful baby boy named Michael Allen, after my father.

Years later when I was diagnosed clinically manic depressive,

I would have to take medication for the rest of my life. If I decided to have a child, it was probable that the child would not be normal. That was devastating news and adoption was not something I considered.

14

So Many Men, So Much Disappointment

I left my mother's apartment and moved into a small cabin behind an elderly woman's house in downtown Miami. The cabin was in a low income section of town but it was convenient to get to work. The most important thing was that I was going to be independent. I could forget about my former relationships. I would finally listen to the doctor's orders and cut the apron strings from my mother. In the cabin, there was a single bed, a toilet, and a small burner to cook on. When you opened the door, you could barely turn around or fit more than one person in at a time. To my surprise, Skippy was anxious to see it, but when he arrived he had tears in his eyes. "Do not worry Skippy, I finally have a place of my own."

He had become a successful businessman, living in a big house in the south Miami area. I still was certain that with each new job and more money, I would be able to improve my living arrangements. I had twelve jobs in the 70's and with each one, I had more responsibility and was rewarded for my increased skills with a higher salary. I was gaining more independence and self esteem. I saw Dr. Slickman once a month and he said that I could slowly reduce my medication.

My life was coming together and I was going to make a commitment. I told myself, "You must become emotionally stable, and stay away from intimate relationships with men."

I was at the receptionist desk of the office where I worked when a new paper goods salesman stood in front of the pass through.

"Good morning, you must be the new receptionist."

"Yes, I started last week." I could barely get the words out. His blonde hair and Paul Newman blue eyes blinded me.

"I am here to stock your inventory."

"Great," I replied. "Please go ahead and let me know if there is anything I need to do."

"Okay," he said, "and I will be back to talk to you when I am finished." He gave me his card and I stared at it for a long time. When he came back, he said, "I am here every two weeks. I don't see a ring on your finger, are you single?"

I thought for a few seconds before I said, "Yes, I am, but I am unavailable."

"That's too bad," he replied, "because you are really cute."

I played it cool for about a month, but every time he came into the office he would compliment me. I finally accepted a date for a simple bicycle ride and picnic. I made the decision that I was going to keep the relationship platonic.

He would tell jokes and make me laugh a lot. It was nice having a guy as a friend for a change. Time passed and his charisma overwhelmed me. My gut feeling told me that this guy was different than the others. He was kind and generous and sensitive. I felt comfortable and safe when we were together. Could this be the one?

We finished making love, he lit a cigarette, and without

looking directly at me, whispered, "You know, Toni, if you lost some weight, I would marry you."

Trying to stay calm, I replied, "Well, I might consider marrying you, if you were a better lover!"

The next day at work, I took 8 reams of 8-1/2 x 11 and shredded them.

When the boss was at lunch, I took 48 rolls of toilet paper and 24 rolls of paper towels and put them in the dumpster. (I saved some toilet paper and paper towels and put them in the trunk of my car.) The next day, I told my boss that there was something wrong with the paper goods delivery and the order was short. They replaced the salesman the following week.

It was in October when I started a telephone flirtation with a customer from New Jersey. We talked for months, but I learned he had never been to Florida. He said he was coming down in the winter and would love to go to Jai Alai. I had never been and it sounded kind of exciting so I accepted. A few days later we were in a motel together. He was older but had money to take me places. One time he came to town and wanted to take a drive down to Key West. We walked around and looked in expensive jewelry stores.

I thought it was odd when he said, "Let's go in. I want to buy something for my wife."

"You never mentioned you had a wife. You cheat on your wife? What's the matter with you?"

He bought her a "guilt necklace." He never offered to buy me anything. I did not let him take advantage of me again. I found his home number and left a "wake up" call for his wife.

"Be aware that your husband does not go to Florida just for business."

End of affair.

Tim was completely different from any man I ever went

out with. He was in the Coast Guard. I met him at the airport on the weekends when I worked part time for a travel agency. My job was to greet cruise passengers, unload baggage and escort them by bus to the pier. He appeared cocky and arrogant at first but he had the cutest "Errol Flynn" like moustache.

He flirted with all the girls and they loved it. He was 6' tall and slim. I was extremely attracted to him but was not sure if I could compete with the other girls. I was not a challenge. He probably could see that I was easy. When he finally asked me out, I was thrilled.

He took me to the Coast Guard lounge on our first date, and it was not long before I knew he had a drinking problem. He kept ordering one rum and coke after another. I had a virgin Bloody Mary (sort of an oxymoron). He lived in a trailer. He had smelly feet in bed but I still did not kick him out of it. Divorced twice he must have had low self esteem. I could relate and sensed that he needed me. Tim was the only man who ever proposed to me, and he was drunk at the time.

After a few months of dating, one of the girls down at the pier approached me and said, "You know, Toni, you are not the only one dating Tim."

"What, I exclaimed!"

"Just ask him."

He was down at the opposite end of the pier. I yelled out and he turned around with a startled look. "What's this I hear about you dating Tina?" He did not deny it. He came over and whispered in my ear, "Toni, you know that you are my favorite fox." I was beginning to wise up. He was just another cheating bastard.

The next morning at work, I received a dozen white roses with a card saying "to my favorite fox."

"You have lying eyes" was Tim's favorite song. He had

them. I was not going to be a fool. I threw the flowers away. I never had to smell those dirty feet again.

I was completely fed up and needed another hiatus from men. I tried very hard to isolate myself from any possible relationships, but my best friend thought I was spending too much time at home and suggested that we go to the "Telephone" lounge for a drink. Reluctantly I agreed. She was a dark-haired beauty who men always found attractive. She never had any problems being picked up at a lounge. I was painfully shy in group settings. A guy would have to approach me and get to know my inner beauty and personality before there was an attraction. This place made it easier.

Each table had a telephone. If you saw someone who caught your eye, you could simply call the table on the phone.

I was pretty sure that my friend would be called, but what a surprise when the phone rang and someone asked to speak to me, "the sweet, young, blonde lady." "How are you all doing tonight, he said in a sexy southern accent?"

"Just fine," I replied (imitating the southern drawl).

"Can I buy you ladies a drink?"

"That would be lovely," I said. "We will have two Singapore Slings."

"Great, I will have them sent over right away and see you all in a few minutes."

He had wavy blonde hair, not too tall, but had nice broad shoulders.

I could tell that he was strong, because his muscles were showing through his short sleeve blue shirt. It was a turn on.

He told me that he was an electrician doing some sub-contractor work in the local area. He did not know how long he would be in town, but he wanted to make some friends. We did become friends and he was a real gentleman. For once, I was treated like a lady and he even introduced me to his family.

Our friendship started to heat up and he became a loving sex partner. I saw him at least twice a week and realized I had to back off a little because it was too good to be true.

After a few weeks of dating, he said that he had to go to Atlanta for an electrician's seminar and would call when he returned. That was the last time I heard from him.

15

Visiting Day

Sunday was visiting day at the Annex. We all waited breathlessly to see if a friend or loved one would show up, but the Annex was not a popular destination. Family would much prefer to go to a psychiatric thriller movie than grace the halls of the Annex. The walls were dark gray and the floors were hard cement. It was cold and smelled of dirty underwear and hospital gowns. I had the feeling that if an outsider came, they may get so depressed they'd have to be committed. Like the characters in the movie "One Flew over the Cuckoo's Nest," they feared the same people who were walking the streets but did not have the good fortune of being locked up.

"You have a visitor, Toni," announced Nurse Hatchet.

"Who could that be?"

I looked down the corridor at the image of a short, well built man with bushy hair and a grey beard. He had pink cheeks and a broad smile. Wow, it was Rob. Was I dreaming? I had not seen him in over five years. He gave me a big bear hug. I was worried how I might look to him. My hair was straggly and I was wearing an old robe. Rob was the kind of guy who wouldn't care. He was a warm and lovable person.

"How did you find me?"

"I ran across one of your neighbors and she told me." Rob was a recovering alcoholic and understood what it meant to have someone support them in a time of need.

For a short time in the 70's, he was my lover and friend. We broke up because he felt that being twenty years my senior was too old. He gave me the book "Be Here Now" which I read daily and cherished as much as someone reading the verses from the Bible.

I found out he was a gourmet cook for rock groups when we met in line at a health food store. He was buying lots of fruits and vegetables. He looked like a hippie with his long bushy hair and was barefoot. He was a free spirit and there was an immediate attraction.

I spent one of the most exciting, adventurous, romantic, spiritual and tumultuous months of my life with Rob. I truly believed that he knew my thoughts and feelings better than any other friend I had. He had an incredible gift of unconditional love. No matter what path he took, Rob left an impression that was surely unforgettable. I fell in love with him the first night we spent together. He dressed like a bohemian, he was always in need of a haircut and getting his beard groomed, but this man had more sex appeal in his pinky than most men have in their entire bodies.

He was wise yet also extremely emotionally insecure. He loved to laugh. He was polygamous and never tried to hide it. He was always late. He hated politics. He was a non-conformist who followed the teachings of a guru. He was non-materialist and had an insatiable appetite for pleasing women in every way. He was unpredictable and spontaneous. He was previously married and had two children but hated long term commitment and the responsibilities that went with it. He told me that he was from Cleveland and he was Paul Newman's college roommate in Ohio. It did not matter if it was true or not; when he told me I believed him.

Rob was without doubt the most romantic man I had ever known. It did not matter if we never went out for an expensive dinner. He left notes in my apartment when I was sleeping. I recalled one particular day when I woke up and there were all these yellow post-it-notes all over the living room with a single word on each note. He liked the way I kept my house clean and organized. When I arranged the notes on the dining room table, they spelled out "You are a very, very, neat person in every way."

He made me feel like the most special person in the world. Another day, I came home and there was a clear margarine top at the back door with the words inscribed "sailed by and thinking of you."

The back door faced the Inter coastal waterway. He was able to sail up to the apartment house and climb up the back porch. Before I met this special man, he had another life. He had been married, had two older sons, and had a girlfriend with a baby boy out of wedlock. He did not talk much about them but only that he did not want to be committed again. He appeared at times to show some guilt about not spending more time with his children. When I was with him, I was the only woman in his life.

Rob's living quarters were on the grounds of a private home where the rock groups stayed when they arrived in Florida.

His tiny living quarters reflected his personality completely. He had lots of plants which were overgrown and neglected, because he did not spend much time there. He hung some of his clothes on hooks and the rest were thrown on a chair. His philosophy was to earn enough money to travel and sail. When he ran out of money he would always find another job. Making love was joyful but if the phone rang he always told the person at the other end "I love you too." This would make me feel jealous but Rob used the word 'love' very loosely.

One night he stayed over at the apartment, and we awoke to his former girlfriend standing in front of us with the baby in her arms.

"Rob," I screamed, "how did she get in here?" He said she knew where I lived and we probably left the back door open by mistake. Both of us were in shock. He sent me to the bathroom and when he came to get me they were gone. I then realized his lack of responsibility and moral integrity. Although I felt sorry for his ex-girlfriend, I was still in love with him.

In many ways, Rob's personality was similar to mine. Recovering alcoholics and manic depressives seem to share a lot in common. We were unstable, reckless and definitely had enormous sexual appetites.

In the summer of '79, Rob and I went on a week's vacation in St. Thomas. He was hired to sail and cook aboard a wealthy couple's 53 foot sailing vessel. He could use it when they were out of the country. He invited me to come along and I would pay my own air fare. He'd provide the three F's: food, fun and fucking. I happily accepted the invitation. We sailed to St. Johns beach and took off our clothes and hung them on the branch of a tree. For three days straight, we made passionate love in the sand while listening to the sounds of the sea. We walked among goats and took pictures with the natives. Rob made the most scrumptious dinners with fresh caught fish and produce from the local markets.

It was a wonderful weekend and aside from the occasional

nausea while sailing, Rob gave me a little souvenir to take home. I contracted a yeast infection.

Rob would not be home for several months so he asked me to stop by his place to water his plants. One Sunday, when I went to his apartment, I was surprised to find another woman watering the plants. "Hi, my name is Toni, what's yours?"

"Sue," she replied.

"Well, Sue, it looks like we both are helping Rob out while he is away. I just got back from a week sailing with him and he asked me to come by to water his plants."

We both were shocked. "What?" exclaimed Sue, "I was there the week before and I guess we both have been fucked!"

When Rob returned at the end of the summer, he called me. "What were you thinking, Rob? Do you really think you can always get away with deceiving innocent women because you are so charming?"

He replied, "Toni, I hate what I am doing to you. I am too old and crazy for you, and you deserve someone who can give you what you need."

I knew he was right. Even though it hurt, it was time to move on. We never discussed Sue further. I decided that he would have to handle that alone. He did not want to end it over the phone, so we agreed to meet. That is when he handed me the book, "Be Here Now." It was the end of another affair, but he would remain in my heart forever.

We hugged goodbye and he walked down the long hall. As he waved goodbye, he said, "Don't ever forget (be here now) this is only a temporary situation. Take this time to reflect on the things that you would like to change and go forward. The future is yours, baby, and I love you."

I remembered my recent dream. His visit was definitely spiritual.

When I recall all the chances I took in those days, I wonder how I did not get into more trouble.

Clara wanted to know where my brother and his family were during all of these trials and tribulations. She did not understand why Skippy did not come to visit me.

I explained that he always felt somewhat indifferent to me and my mother. He was a domestic kind of guy who supported his wife and enabled his two adopted children. I defended his behavior, but deep down was hurt. He was never demonstrative of his feelings. Then again, neither was my mother.

I tried to make excuses and accept their lack of affection. Skippy had his family responsibilities and may have felt that he was going to be burdened with taking care of a sick mother and sister after my father died. I told myself that perhaps his tour in Vietnam had hardened him. It would always remain an unresolved issue that I'd have to accept and learn to live with.

I was learning from therapy that I had to be independent and strong. No one else could do that for me. With friends, a good support system and daily medication, there was no reason I could not live a successful and happy life.

"That's enough about my family for now, Clara. Let's go back to the men in my life. That is way more exciting."

There was one guy who actually could have been a good partner for me, but I was too immature and picky to realize what I could have had. It was the evening I took a non-credit class at a local high school. This guy sat in front of me and the teacher asked a question. I answered and he turned around to get a look at me. He smiled and said, "I like the sound of your voice."

I liked his Kenny Rogers look, with a well trimmed beard, until he stood up and was about 5' 2" in height. Oh no! No way that I could go out with a man two and one-half inches shorter than me. Then I thought of Elizabeth Taylor and Mickey Rooney. If it was good enough for them, who was I to be so superficial?

He asked, "What is your favorite food?" He wanted to take me to dinner and I could not resist his offer. "Duck with cherry sauce."

He knew just the right place to take me and was making a very good first impression. His kindness and thoughtfulness were refreshing. He tried to please me in every way. He was a good person and became a wonderful friend.

Too bad he lacked ambition and only had a high school education. He could only get menial jobs and was a school sanitation worker. I knew that it was not nice to use him as a meal ticket but he was crazy about me. He lived with his mother and every extra dollar he earned was spent on our dates. His hobby was going to the Miami Dolphin's football games. They bored me, but to please him I went sporting a Dolphin t-shirt and hat. In college, I learned how to scream and stand up with the crowd. You should have seen me yelling, "First and ten, do it again, harder, harder" (As if I knew what was happening). You could tell by the big smile on his face just how happy he was.

We spent a lot of time going to the beach. Like every relationship, there were problems. When I tried to encourage him to further his career, he did not appear to be interested. These were the type of men I always seemed to attract. Who was I to be giving advice? I hoped for a man who could support me emotionally as well as financially. I was having a difficult time accepting his "shortcomings." When I convinced him to try for a better position at the school, he wore a suit which was two sizes too large. When we went swimming, halfway out in the ocean waves, you could see his head disappearing as he came closer to me.

When we made love, his tiny hands turned me off. The night he told me he was in love, I broke it off. I may have lost the only man who really loved me.

Suddenly, Nurse Hatchit shouted out to the group.

"Get ready, girls and boys, we are going for a walk in the park." I was looking forward to seeing the little beige and white puppy that was there the last time we went to the park. He was so friendly and adorable. Someday, I hoped to get a dog of my own. I always longed to own one. I could hear my mother say to me, "Toni, as long as we live in an apartment you can only have a bird, a turtle or some fish."

"How am I going to play with them?"

Getting a dog would be a priority when I lived on my own.

"Look, Clara, he's running across the grass directly toward me. Hi, little one, how are you today? Oh, you are such a sweet thing."

"Do you want to hold him?" said the kind gentleman.

"Yes, I would love to." I picked him up and placed his tiny soft and fuzzy head on my chest. He had the most loving big brown eyes and felt warm like a baby. "What's his name?"

"Andy," said the gentleman.

"That's a nice name," I said." "He is a special little guy, and I hope that someday I can have a puppy just like him."

"If you believe, then you will."

The kind gentleman had a white beard. He wore a red tee shirt with the logo "Dog Walkers of America," blue jeans and suspenders with tiny flowers. He spoke softly, and had a warm smile. He appeared to be in his late 50s and reminded me of Rob. "Do you come to the park often?"

"Oh yes, at least three times a week. My puppy and I love nature." I thought about what he said and how much I missed being outside among the trees, the flowers and the sunshine.

The next morning, a large bouquet of sunflowers with wild flowers arrived in a crystal vase.

They were delivered to my room. I loved the array of bright yellow, blue and lavender colors. They reminded me of the French countryside which I had seen in a magazine. They had the aroma of fresh air. The card read "From an admirer." "Come here quickly, Clara."

"Do you think that kind gentleman from the park sent these flowers?"

"Could be," she replied.

"Look, there is more on the back of the card," I said. "We hope that you will someday be in a garden surrounded by a field of flowers as beautiful as you."

"How sweet his words awere," I thought.

It was going to be a week before we went back to the park and I had no other way to thank him for the flowers. I had nightly dreams about seeing them again. Weeks came and went. There was no sign of Andy or his owner when we returned to the park. I took his card, folded it in half, and stuck it in the pants pocket of my favorite jeans for safekeeping.

Dr. Rosen was preparing for my departure from the hospital. He assigned me a project. I had to apply and be hired for a job before being dispatched. That was a tall order. My typing skills were shaky and I was nervous. They brought in a new electric typewriter, and I practiced for one hour each day.

I found out that typing is like driving a car. You never really forget. After three weeks, Dr. Rosen was pleased with my progress. When my lithium dosage was regulated, and I was beginning to stabilize, he brought me the Herald every day to look for a job.

Dr. Rosen warned me of the side effects of the medication. "It will be worth it," he assured me, "but do not go off of your medication or you will suffer the consequences. Your manic depressive symptoms will reappear or even get worse. The medication passes through the kidneys and we will do periodic blood work to test your kidney levels. If the levels are elevated, we will adjust or change your medications.

"The most important thing you should know is that there is no reason for you not to have a completely happy and productive life. You are responsible for your choices and actions. You have come such a long way while you have been here and I will be here for you as long as you need me."

16

Looking for a Job

I searched the classifieds and the phone book, writing down the names and phone numbers of local temporary agencies and called to make appointments. Each day, I was allowed to go to one agency and then report back immediately. I was sure they would send a bounty hunter if I did not show up in a few hours. Fortunately, the first temporary agency hired me.

"Wow, this is much easier than I thought it would be." It was a secretarial position with a large telecommunications company that offered a competitive salary and, if things worked out, the possibility of being hired permanently. I began to notice the weight gain.

This may have been due to all of the tuna fish subs I was consuming. Clara left the hospital the week before and I wished her all the best. She said that she was going to try to work hard at staying married and would have me over for dinner real soon. The hospital arranged for me to continue to see Dr. Rosen on a monthly basis and he would monitor my lithium.

The first day on the job, I could barely contain myself.

I checked in with Clara every week, and we spoke for hours. She was pleased that she'd made a friend for life.

I worked hard and learned all that I could about the industry. I developed a mild crush on my boss who was single and very handsome. He traveled often, but we spoke on the phone almost every day.

He always came back from trips with small tokens of appreciation. He acknowledged my birthday and Secretary's Day. After about six months, he appeared comfortable enough with me to say, "Toni, if you lose twenty pounds, I will give you a free weekend to Disney World." What was wrong with men? Why couldn't I just be accepted for who I am? I swore that I would never let anyone try to change me.

From that day forward, I concentrated on becoming more successful in my career. My hard work and long hours paid off. I was promoted to being a customer trainer after three years. I traveled throughout the Southeast and trained customers in telecommunications. I was visiting areas that I would never have gone if it were not for the job.

Some of the trainings were so unique, like the time I had to drive over two hours to a small town outside of Alabama to a women's correctional facility. I trained the head secretary on a telex machine (like a teletype) which was the prevalent choice of communications between companies. The corrections officer took me for a tour through the area where they housed the criminally insane. If she only knew that I was formerly an inmate at the Annex!

My primary job was to prepare personalized training guides for the company's top revenue-producing accounts. The best part was I would schedule my arrival in a city on Sunday so that I could have at least one day to explore the area.

Bosses never questioned budgets or schedules, as long as

the jobs were completed. Each trip was more exciting than the last.

There was little time for social commitment back home. As far as dating, this was probably a good thing, but even seeing female friends was very difficult to schedule.

In the interim, my mother's health was failing. For years I would hear her say,

"Toni, I wish that I could just close my eyes and never wake up." I felt enormous pain when she uttered these words. But what could I do for her?

My aunt tried to cook healthy meals for her but I watched her take her food and place it in a napkin under the table.

Due to the build up of phlegm, once a month she was hospitalized to have her lungs cleaned out. She was growing weaker and was 72 pounds when she passed. On her death certificate, it said she died of malnutrition. I remember arriving at their apartment to see her taken to the funeral home. She received a graveside burial with just a few relatives attending. I know that she was ready and in reality I was relieved too.

Around the time my mother died, my father's sister left Skippy and me a large inheritance. We always knew that there was a trust in our names, and I was convinced that my mother was getting ready to pass on when she realized that I would be financially taken care of. I may not have felt very close to my mother in life, but I felt closer in death.

17

Job Transfer

About a month after my mother passed on, my boss approached me and said, "There is a position open in the Northeast that we would like to offer to you. Would you be interested in transferring? We will pay your moving expenses and you will get an automatic five percent pay increase."

It did not seem like much, but I was thrilled that they were considering me.

The timing was good, since my mother had passed. I hoped it was not the New York area. I grew up there and did not want to go back.

There were too many bad memories. "Where in the Northeast?" I asked.

"Boston," he replied. I was thrilled. I always wanted to visit New England and this was an opportunity I might not receive again. I had no strong ties in Florida accept for an occasional visit to my brother. For the most part, we only got together on Jewish holidays.

One of my friends said, "Oh, you have to buy a mink coat if you are going to the Northeast. It is frigid in the winter. It's the thing, everyone has one, you know."

That weekend, I went to the fur store at the mall and purchased a beautiful mink jacket with fox trim.

When I arrived in Boston, the terminal was bustling. It had been almost nineteen years since I'd been up north. The change would be good, once I got used to the freezing cold weather. I was already imagining all of the wonderful places I would see in New England. Back home, when I had little money to travel, I would watch the travel channel and dream of all the places I might visit one day. It was now becoming a reality. I reflected back to my days in the hospital and felt so blessed.

The local support representative, Jackie, was waiting for me in the baggage claim area.

"Welcome to Boston, Toni, how was your trip?"

"Just wonderful," I replied.

"We will be putting you up at a hotel in the area, but first I am going to show you around some areas in downtown and on the north shore, so that you can see where you might like to live."

"I did a little homework before I came and brought a newspaper article on a luxury apartment in the north area. "I would love to see the brownstones in the Back Bay, if that is possible."

"Absolutely, let's be on our way."

The streets of downtown Boston were very quaint, lined with beautiful shops and trendy restaurants. I imagined living in a brownstone but the parking was extremely impractical.

Only one parking space was allowed to each house. It would be almost impossible for them to find a space any time of the day especially during rush hour.

"Okay, let's drive north," Jackie said. "That's where I live and it is only twenty minutes from the office. I think you will like it."

"The drivers in Boston are a lot worse than Florida," I

exclaimed. I held on tight as Jacque barreled her way through the tunnels on I-93.

I was relieved when we got off the main highway and started driving past a beautiful State Park that seemed to go on for miles. Jacque said it was actually seven miles to the borders of the area she thought I might like.

I was amazed at all of the large trees and colorful foliage that lined the streets of the magnificent colonial and Victorian homes. Everything was so quaint. It was such a nice change from Florida and the palm trees. It was love at first sight and I immediately felt a sense of warmth and belonging. Jacque took a slight turn so that we could go the scenic route. This took us through the downtown area which was a picture perfect village with its cobblestone streets, small boutiques, antique shop, country French kitchen store, homemade bakery, and a few small family style restaurants where everybody knew each other.

There was a beautiful common area with majestic trees where people were walking their dogs while children played in the snow.

That afternoon, I signed a lease with an apartment house in the north just outside of the downtown area and contacted a moving company to make arrangements to have my belongings shipped as soon as possible.

When I moved into my new home, I decided to check out the clubhouse to see what was going on. When I walked in, several women were listening to a man giving a lecture on the Art of Massage. How perfect. He was a gorgeous Italian with dark curly hair, dark brown eyes and a full dark beard.

What a hunk. His voice was very soft and he intrigued me. After he was finished with his lecture, I approached him and asked him if he gives massages in the home.

"Of course, I do. My name is Victor. What's yours, lovely lady?"

"It's Toni and I just moved into this building. I have not had a massage in a long time, but I really could use one. I have been under a lot of stress lately." I took his card and when I got home I immediately called to set up an appointment for the following Monday evening. I thought about Victor and the massage all week. When Monday came, I prepared the house for his arrival.

I put on soft music, lit candles, and sprayed some perfume on the night table bulb which was near the area where I would ask him to place his table.

When the door opened, he smiled and he had the largest cleft dimple I had ever seen in a man. He was truly handsome. I offered him a cup of hot green tea but he only wanted a glass of water. He neatly placed a sheet and blanket on the table and said we would begin with me lying on my stomach. He covered me and then slowly pulled down the sheet from my back. He applied warm oil and began to massage my back. His hands were soft as he moved them across my shoulders, neck and down my spine.

The scent of the aromatherapy oil was intoxicating. I was tingling. He kept reminding me to relax, but it was difficult. I wanted to turn over and attack him. After he completed my back side, I turned over and he softly pressed his hands on my upper chest, then my arms, hands, fingers, legs and spent extra time on my feet. All of the time, he was a perfect gentleman. I was floating. When he said "time is up," I did not want it to end.

"You were wonderful, Victor. Same time next week, please."

It became a standing appointment. Victor and I became good friends but I secretly wanted to be more than friends.

I bought him presents and made dinner for him on his birthday. He was always very grateful. He invited me to his parties, but he had a girlfriend much younger than me. I fantasized that he would fall in love with me, and continuously called him on the phone to get his attention. After one massage, I agonized over our friendship. As he was leaving, I blurted out,

"I love you, please, Victor, and I do not want you to leave."

His reply was, "I love you as a person, but I am not in love with you."

I was so hurt and embarrassed I did not try to contact him after that. I never heard from him again.

I was always sorry for the friendship that I screwed up. The next morning I went into Woburn office teary-eyed. I already knew some of the sales people because they were at meetings that I had attended. It appeared that my colleagues thought I was some kind of a "rich bitch" when I walked into the office.

"Is that coat real?" asked one of the girls.

"Yes, of course," I said. "Is there a problem?"

"A little fancy for work, don't you think?"

"A friend in Florida told me that everyone in Boston owns a fur."

The girls all laughed. I had been made a fool of the first day, but I was determined to fit in. I was going to work my butt off and impress the district manager.

After a year of living in my apartment, I decided that I really wanted to buy a home. I had never owned anything in my life, but now I was finally in a position to buy. There was a new development of thirty-nine beautiful California-style townhomes being built diagonally across the street from my apartments. When they went on the market, I quickly grabbed the most desirable location. The back of the house faced part of the state park on a private college campus. It was gorgeous.

When all the units were sold, the developer went into bankruptcy. Every winter, the owners were responsible for finding a contractor to remove snow from the roofs and the homeowner association assessments were getting very expensive.

When the home market was in trouble, a new developer bought those in foreclosure at a very low price. That lowered the value of the houses dramatically. I was not about to move. I loved the house and was willing to pay whatever it cost to stay there. In order to make my life complete, my dream of owning a dog was about to become real. I wanted a small puppy, so I did some research on the best dog for a single person who worked full time. The "Shih Tzu" was a very popular breed. There was a breeder south of Boston.

I drove down that weekend.

There was a darling beige and white mixed breed puppy with his tail wagging. I picked him up in my arms and knew he would be my baby boy. I took him to the vet to be checked out. When he said "You've got a good one," I took him home, named him "Charlie Chan" and then shortened it to "Charlie."

Everyone in the neighborhood knew and loved him for his sweet demeanor. He was my buddy and he brought me love that I never knew I could feel for any living animal. After a few months of being settled in my new home, my boss came to me and said, "You are doing such a wonderful job, we would like you to support our largest customer and that would mean working onsite at their location thirty miles south of where you live."

It was Murphy's Law but I knew it was it was a wonderful opportunity and learning experience.

Every Monday morning, I went into the office for a meeting. "Today we announce the candidates for Sales Support Representative of the Year," he said.

You cannot imagine my surprise when he said, "Toni, you have been chosen as representative of the year for the international division for your outstanding service and support." I was up against some very capable support people who had a lot more knowledge and years of service than I.

Being humble, I thought that it must have been politically motivated because I supported their largest revenue producer. However, I was extremely honored, not to mention, that I had also worked my butt off, figuratively speaking.

For the next few years, I continued to plan and manage the company's communications gateway onsite. It was a challenging and rewarding position. I also became friendly with my peer group and we socialized when we were not working. I was very happy in New England. I missed Florida only during the months of January, February and March when the temperatures were usually below the teens. Skippy managed to visit one time with his family. They really hated the cold weather.

I was planning seminars and receiving sales support awards. For the first time in my life, I had reached the pinnacle of success in my career. My peers accepted me for who I was even with a few extra pounds. My social life was less than desirable, but I had my work, my home, and most of all a beautiful puppy.

18

Lonely in New England

Holidays were lonely and, after a year in New England, I thought that it might be an appropriate time to start making more friends and dating again. A good safe place to start would be the Jewish Community Center. They had a social group for people over forty. They organized the kinds of events I enjoyed which included movies, dinner and cocktail parties. There was a "Welcome Party" for newcomers in the area. I decided to go. I saw a very interesting-looking guy standing in the corner talking to a group of women. He was definitely someone I could be attracted to. He was very tall with a big frame.

Since I had gained weight, I felt more comfortable with men who had a little meat on their bones as long as they were well groomed. He came over to talk to me. He liked to talk about philosophical subjects, which interested me. He had a trust fund and did not need to work. He had a dry sense of humor which made me laugh. It had been a long time since I felt a spark. People at the party seemed to know who he was and several of the women watched as we talked. It felt good to have someone giving me attention for a change. He took my phone number and called me the next day. I was impressed. I seldom met men in an environment such as this and I was especially pleased that he would choose me over a number of very attractive ladies.

He made a date and he arrived with my favorite (Chinese food).

As we ate, he began to make critical remarks. First, he asked technical questions about my stereo system. When I did not know the answers, he said, "What, didn't you read the manual?"

I did not know how to reply. Then he asked me for some ice for his drink, and when there wasn't any left in the ice maker, he said, "Don't you have the bar in the right position so it will make ice continuously?"

I thought, who is this guy? He is a real weirdo.

Then while he was eating, I took the empty food boxes and threw them in the garbage. He became outraged and shouted, "Don't throw those out. I may want to take leftovers home."

I was not sure what this man was capable of. He could be a murderer

for all I knew. I sure was not a very good judge of character. I politely asked him to finish his meal and then leave. On the way out he said, "I'll call you."

Don't do me any favors, I thought.

The next day he sent flowers and left three telephone messages. At first, I ignored them.

After his fourth phone call, he apologized profusely and swore he would make it up to me. He invited me to his house for a game of croquet and we could prepare dinner together.

It sounded like fun and I decided to give him another chance. I had never played the game of croquet. From the moment we began, he criticized everything I did. "You do not even know how to hold the mallet," he blurted out.

"What can you expect since I never played before?" I could see what I was getting myself into. He became angry and frustrated and would not even give me the chance.

"Since you obviously cannot play, let's make dinner." He criticized the way I "shucked" the corn.

"Shuck you, baby!" (I mumbled under my breath for fear he would throw something at me). I ran out the kitchen door, got into my car and went home.

Even if it meant that I would never have a date, I wasn't going back to the JCC events. It was one of the most exasperating experiences of my life.

I decided he was the strangest man I had ever met. Yet he continued to call and leave messages. He even tried to call my friends to say how sorry he was and he would make it up to me. I swore from that day forward that I would not be so naïve and would be much more discriminating. With all of the experiences I had in my past, you would think I could see the red flags. When it came to men, I was still careless and vulnerable.

The one guy I could count on was Charlie. "Come on, baby, I know it's freezing out. Let's put on your blue fleece lined jacket and little rubber booties. I have my nice warm mink jacket. I promise it will be a quick walk."

Charlie looked up at me with his adoring eyes as if to say, "Mommy, I wish the snow would melt." One thing for sure was that my heart melted every time he looked at me.

In addition to my career, Charlie was now the most important part of my life. I finally knew unconditional love and I was at peace with myself for the first time.

I realized that I did not need a man, or my mother, to validate my worth. The only immediate issue I had to face would be how to improve my relationship with my brother and my family in Florida. It was time to let go of any hurt feelings and think about the future. They probably were not aware how much I needed family now. No matter how independent I was. Most of all, I needed to know my brother loved me.

19

Going Home

The phone rang. "Hi, it's Skippy."

"Oh, that is so funny, I was just dreaming about you."

"I hope it was a good one. How are you and Charlie doing?"

"Great and could not be better."

"I tried you earlier and your voice message said you were out shoveling snow."

"That was meant to be a joke, but it is about ten degrees as we speak."

"I took a short nap and was just going to take Charlie for a walk."

"Must be cold up there, huh, Sis?"

"I think I'll have to plan a trip to see you real soon!"

"Slow down and wait, it may be sooner than you think," he said.

"What is it, is something wrong?"

"Well, not with any of us."

"Come on. Please don't keep me in suspense."

"I picked up the Herald today, and you won't believe what I read!"

"What?" I exclaimed. I was feeling quite nervous.

"Someone you know very well committed suicide yesterday morning."

I could not imagine who that could be.

"It's right here on the front page of the local news," he said. "Prominent psychiatrist commits suicide."

"Oh my god, it's Dr. Slickman?"

"I'm afraid so, sis."

I was stunned. "Why?"

"We don't know any of the details. The paper only stated it was under investigation."

I was speechless and sad at the same time. This was the doctor who thought he could make me well. This was the same doctor who called me "stupid" for attempting suicide. Now he had fallen from grace.

After a few moments, I felt a tremendous sense of grief. He must have been in a lot pain. He always appeared so cool. His advice to break away from my mother's apron strings still haunted me.

His tough love actually may have helped even though I did not realize it at the time. He could not help himself but I was lucky enough to be alive. What an irony.

I thanked Skippy for calling and hung up the phone.

I was compelled to book a flight to Florida. My plan was to go to the graveside ceremony and call Skippy when I arrived.

I needed closure. Charlie would be able to come for an additional $150.00 and I was told he could be put under my seat in a carrier. When we arrived at the gate, they took one look at Charlie and upgraded us to first class. He sat on my lap like a baby the whole flight. The graveside was adorned with the most beautiful foliage I had ever seen. Dozens of multicolored wild flowers adorned the area and were placed on his casket. At least if the doctor was not happy in his life, he was being laid to rest in a very special place.

Hundreds of friends, family, associates and former patients were paying their respects. I turned around and standing behind a large pine tree was the shadow of a man humming very softly. It sounded like "Kisses Sweeter than Wine." When I looked back, he was gone. Did I imagine something? As the ceremony began, I got a little teary-eyed. I placed my hand in my jeans pocket to get a tissue and pulled out a crumbled piece of paper. It read, "We hope that you will someday be in a garden surrounded by a field of flowers as beautiful as you." Was my mind playing tricks?

Who was the stranger behind the tree? Perhaps one day I will find out, but I know for certain that every day there is a new experience and a new opportunity. I have learned to live in an imperfect world, accept my illness, and I will always appreciate the unexpected beauty that surrounds me.

As I watched them place the body into the ground, I knew there was one thing we had in common. We were at peace. I bowed my head in prayer, and thought, "Who's Stupid Now?"

Epilogue: What Is This Illness?

Individuals with manic depression or bipolar illness have extreme highs and lows. They may be risk takers. They may be adventurous. They may be thrill seekers. Many are over sexed. It is a mental illness with personality disorders. It is a combination of biological, genetic and environmental conditions. It needs to be treated with medication and therapy in order for the individual to be stable and live a healthy life.

It is a very complicated illness and takes many forms. In my case, I believe that I always needed something to satisfy my appetite. If it was not food, then sex. If it was not sex, then love.

If it was not love, it was material things. That is what it boiled down to. And all the searching in the world could not buy the ultimate happiness unless I could feel it within. I needed guidance and the proper prescription to get stabilized.

When I look back at my past behavior, I certainly do not condone it. I would never take the same risks today. Fortunately, I have learned from them and have matured. It was all part of the growing process, and I knew that in the long run it was going to make me a better and stronger person. I refused to use the illness as an excuse. I saw it as an opportunity to accept whatever life challenges were going to come my way.

Perhaps a crucial turning point was the challenge to get through the time at the Annex and leave healthy so I would never have to set foot in a psychiatric hospital again. I knew that I was going to need a good support system, and it started with friends.